Restaurant Business Plan

How to Open a Restaurant Startup and Be Profitable Within the First Year

by Cory Sutherland

Table of Contents

Introduction

If you want to be a successful restaurateur, you're going to need to be hardworking, informed, and fiercely optimistic. The restaurant industry is clouded in an unhealthy and unwarranted pessimism. Brace yourself for the naysayers, who will try to spook you at every turn by bemoaning the industry's "small profit margins" and "high turnover rates." Also, prepare to be confronted time and again with the sour adage proclaiming that "9 out of 10 restaurants fail."

This pessimism is partly nonsensical hype and partly a hazy reflection of what's a genuinely competitive and stressful industry. There is no statistical evidence indicating that 9 out of 10 restaurants fail. In fact, a recent study at Ohio State University found that the success rates of restaurant startups are essentially the same as the rates for other start-up businesses, with about 6 out of 10 new restaurants shutting down operations within the first year. That doesn't mean that being a restaurateur is easy, but it's not as impossible as you've been led to believe.

The most common reasons why restaurants fail are (1) lack of work ethic or passion, (2) lack of sufficient start-up capital, and (3) lack of knowledge and industry experience, not necessarily in order. The restaurant industry rewards only those who have a burning desire to be successful. Not moonlighters and certainly not those who approach the industry looking for easy money. If you're not ready to work, then turn back now. Many would-be restaurateurs, even those with adequate know-how, end up shutting down operations after coming to terms with how much of their time and energy is going to be sacrificed for the business. If you have small children, or if you enjoy the regular golf game or have other hobbies that you really enjoy, prepare to make some sacrifices, especially if you want to turn in a profit the first year.

Expenses add up quickly and banks can be stingy when awarding start-up capital. Some speculate that the banking industry is largely responsible for keeping the "9 out of 10" myth afloat. Perpetuating such a dismal industry track record leads banks to insist on exorbitant interest rates and stingy start-up allocations. The restaurateur, rather than settling for a sub-par loan, would be wise to shop far and wide for competitive capital offers and opportunities, and to be armed with a rock solid business plan that adequately accounts for the many expenses incumbent to owning a restaurant. We'll talk more about financing for your restaurant in Chapter 1.

As for industry knowledge and experience, the more time you spend planning for and running your restaurant, the better you'll get at it. Reading this book will give you an essential head start as you begin your journey to success and profitability. The following chapters will introduce you to the core principles and challenges of starting and owning a successful restaurant startup. Understanding and following the guidelines in this book will ensure your restaurant not only succeeds, but achieves profitability within the first year of its operation!

5

Chapter 1: Designing a Sound Plan to Get Solid Financial Backing

Given that banks are determined to see the restaurant industry as high-risk and only worthy of the most cumbersome and expensive capital investments, how does the would-be restaurateur approach the problem of financing?

It begins, of course, with an expert business plan. Your business plan will provide immeasurable value to your endeavor and will increase your chances of success right out of the gate! Committing several hours, weeks, and even months to the planning process is the first step to making sure that your restaurant is admitted into that upper 40% of successful endeavors.

Among its many benefits, planning will allow you to determine exactly how much money you will need to start your restaurant and keep it afloat until it begins to pay for its own expenses. It's critical that you know your restaurant's up-front cash requirements. Banks will often loan out restaurateurs less than what they need, either because the bank doesn't want to put more money at risk, or because the restaurateur is without adequate collateral, or because the restaurateur hasn't planned appropriately and requests an inadequate sum. One of the most common reasons for a restaurant to fail is lack of sufficient start-up capital. The good news is that you can circumvent this major pitfall easily by putting together a great business plan and knowing exactly how much start-up capital your restaurant will require. Knowing your financial requirements up-front will prevent you from being reckless. Don't start spending until you've got all the cash you need on-hand and ready to deploy. If the bank alone isn't going to be able to float all your bills, then you'll need to look into other sources of start-up funds, including:

Personal Assets and Home Equity — Home value and other personal assets can help you generate immediate cash or the collateral necessary to obtain an adequate loan. If you're serious about owning a restaurant, maybe it's time to sell the speedboat. You probably won't have much time to enjoy it anyways, at least not during the early stages of building your business, and hopefully by the time your restaurant really takes off, you'll be in a position to buy something newer and nicer.

Loans from Friends and Family — If you've got a rock-solid business plan, friends and family who believe in you, and the means to support your endeavor, then by all means ask for that support! That said, don't take close family relationships or friendships for granted.

You owe it to your family members and friends, and to yourself as well, to lay out a detailed assessment of what you need and how you're going to use it to ultimately bring in profit.

Government Assistance — Believe it or not, the government wants you to succeed. The more money you make, the more tax revenue is collected. Look into government programs that support and finance small businesses. Again, you need to have a plan at the ready, as no government endeavor is inclined to hand out cash to an entrepreneur who doesn't already have her act together on paper.

Partners — Maybe you know someone else interested in making a play in the restaurant industry who's got some disposable cash on hand. Maybe there's someone you can find who has a dream of opening a restaurant similar to yours and may want to get his hands dirty with you. Be careful when crafting a partnership, though, and be aware that partnerships take many different forms. Some partners may want to contribute money but have little or nothing to do with the day-to-day operations of the business. If this is the case make sure it's clear as day from the get-go who's entitled to what and always make sure that it's written down on paper. If you're the one doing all the work but only own 50% of the business, then you should require adequate compensation—in the form of a manager's salary perhaps—in addition to your ownership stake.

The seed of your business plan is your restaurant's *concept*. This is your vision for the restaurant's look, feel, and *taste*. What kind of restaurant are you opening? What types of clientele are you going to attract? How expensive is your menu? Are you going to serve alcohol and if so, what additional licensure and start-up expense will you need to prepare for? What type of dining furniture will you require and what is the nature of your restaurant's interior and exterior decorations? How many guests can be seated in your dining area? How many guests are you going to be serving on an average weekend? How many on a weekday? How much service staff will your restaurant require? What meals will your restaurant serve? Which restaurants are your competitors? Which restaurants do you aspire to emulate?

After you have a clear idea of your concept, the other variables will become clearer as well. Let's say, for example, that your concept is a seafood dinner restaurant scaled to a clientele of average household incomes. Your menu is $15-$20 per entrée, and you've decided on ten dishes that you definitely want to offer your guests. How does this concept affect other decisions you need to make? How experienced and talented does your chef need to be? Who are your wholesale food distributors and how expensive are they? Are you going to need to invest in new or used equipment, refrigerators, ranges, dishwashers, serving trays, silverware etc? What will be required in the way of furniture and decoration? Spend the time to refine and understand your restaurant's concept, and the start-up financial requirements will steadily fall into place.

Once you know your start up expense, calculate your day-to-day static operating expenses. Static operating expenses refer to expenditures that will stay constant (or static) regardless of sales volume. For example, your wholesale food costs are dynamic operating expenses since they fluctuate in direct proportion to your sales volume. Static operating expenses include your staff members' salaries, your rent and utilities, equipment maintenance expense, insurance, any refreshable décor items such as flowers, candles, lightbulbs, and disposable items such as napkins, garbage bags, and receipt paper. It's important to keep your accounting as detailed as possible because you will inevitably encounter unforeseen expenses that will put unexpected strain on your planned budget.

After you understand your restaurant's static expenses, you'll need to start considering your variable expenses. Food and beverage costs will be your main variable expense as well as staffing, which we'll talk about more in Chapter 4. Food and beverage costs should come to, on average, 28% to 35% of the overall operating budget for the business, with smaller restaurants landing on the lower end of the spread.

You can model your food and beverage expense by estimating your sales volume and gross profit. Gross profit is the sales value minus the cost of goods sold. You can estimate your gross profit by figuring out how many customers you expect to serve on a weekly basis. Naturally, if you plan on being successful, you'll want to assume that you're going to create positive word-of-mouth for your restaurant and that your customer count on week 30 is going to be a lot higher than it was on week 15. It may be helpful to come up with an average expenditure for your restaurant.

For example, in our seafood restaurant, our entrée sold for $15-$20. Let's assume our average entrée sale is $17.50 and that we sell an average of $5 worth of beverages and $3 worth of appetizers to each customer putting us at a total of $25.50 per customer in total sales. Next we'd calculate an average of the total expense per customer in terms of cost of goods sold (or COGS). In the restaurant industry, COGS is typically known as "usage costs." Let's say your usage cost comes out to be about $10 per customer per visit. Therefore, our total average GP or Gross Profit (sales minus COGS) per customer per visit is $15.50. From here you can get an idea of how many customer visits per month on average you'll need to recoup your static expenses and how much profit you can expect to make and when.

In order to be profitable before the end of your first year in business, you'll need to plan accordingly. Set milestones for the number of guests you expect to eat at your restaurant week by week. If you fall short of your milestone, figure out why. Was the service or the food poor, causing the customer to leave unsatisfied? Do enough people know about your restaurant? As the owner-operator, your job is to continually tweak and fix the weak points in your business and drive the business to profitability.

Chapter 2: Choosing the Ideal Location

Before you can make sound estimates on how busy your restaurant will be, especially in its first several weeks, you'll need to consider and decide on a location. In addition to the concept of your restaurant and choice of chef, choice of location is essential to determining whether your restaurant succeeds or fails.

Restaurant locations come in varying shapes and sizes. Some restaurant locations enjoy parades of heavy foot traffic, while others are secluded to minimize noise and heighten ambiance. Your concept in this sense should influence your choice of location. For example, if you're running a quick service burrito joint, then a wide open entrance in the middle of a heavily trafficked strip mall will do just fine. But if you're thinking tablecloths, tuxedo-clad servers, and fifty-dollar entrées, then you'll probably want a location a bit more reserved and insulated from any distracting thoroughfares.

A good way to get ideas about the optimal location for your restaurant is by visiting other restaurants and taking notes. Do the guests respond well to their environment? Do they look comfortable in their chairs and not cramped for space? Is there adequate dining space available? Does the location fit with the restaurant's concept? You should also take note of the prep and cooking space. Is there adequate room for the cooks to work and for the wait staff to pick up orders? Are there accessible restroom facilities for both guests and staff members? After you scout out each location, assess which elements of this location fit with your restaurant concept and which elements you would approach differently.

You should also be mindful of the type of guest that your concept is going to attract. Simply put, if you open an authentic Chinese restaurant in the heart of Chinatown, it will in most cases fare better than an authentic Greek restaurant in the same location. If you're considering opening up in a shopping mall, then you'll probably want to go in with something middle-of-the-road price-wise and that will appeal to both young adults with little disposable income as well as more affluent clientele. It would be foolish and likely fatal to pay high rent for a heavily trafficked location, only to go in with a concept that excludes major segments of your potential clientele.

Your location needs to be logistically sound. You'll need a backlot of some sort to unload inventory from delivery trucks. You should find out if there are any local ordinances that restrict the times when you can receive shipments. Parking availability can also be a major factor to consider. You'll also need to thoroughly explore your prospective location's interior from front to back. Make sure that there's space inside to store food, a place to collect waste, as well as an external disposal site. Don't forget to provide adequate counter space for cooks to prepare food, as well as a small office for management activities.

Finally, you need to consider the amount of money you'll be spending on rent and whether the restaurant's projected gross profit will adequately pay for this fixed expense. As a best practice, complete your concept first along with a sales-and-profit projection. Even though your location will influence your sales and profits, you should have a general idea of how much revenue your restaurant *concept* can generate before you make a final decision on location. You should have a range of rent costs that your restaurant concept can afford and limit your search to locations within this range. This will be particularly easy to do if you're opening up a franchise restaurant with pre-established gross profit margins. But even if you're creating an original concept, you should still be able to compare yours to others in your region. Find out who's doing well with similar concepts, where they're operating, and how much rent they're paying.

Chapter 3: How to Partner with the Right Chef

Another decision that you must get right if you hope to breach that upper 40% of restaurants which survive the first year is the decision of which chef to hire. The simple two-part version of executive chef selection and retention is as follows:

Step 1: Hire on culture and philosophy. During your chef selection process, you must do everything you can to assess how seamlessly your chef's vision for a successful restaurant overlaps with your own. Sure, you'll have a barrage of other tests to assess competency, but being on the same page philosophically is a must-have.

Step 2: Endow your executive chef with executive responsibilities. The reason it's so important you and your executive chef have a shared vision for your restaurant is because many of the restaurant's creative and financial decisions will fall on the shoulders of your executive chef. For example, if your vision is to run a restaurant that caters to middle-class and frugal clientele but your executive chef believes that no expense should ever be spared when it comes to food, then you're setting yourselves up to butt heads.

These two steps are the essentials of acquiring and managing your executive chef. Other important ways to assess for competency include:

- Have your prospective chefs prepare one of your restaurant's important dishes. Evaluate their work on presentation, preparation time, and of course, taste.

- Have your prospective chef assess a food budget and prepare a dish confined to the cost and quantities specified by the budget. This will allow you to see who understands the importance of minimizing costs and producing menu items that will appeal to more frugal-minded customers.

- Call references. If your prospective chef has been around for a while, he or she should be able to provide references who can attest to their competencies. Pay attention to the longevity of previous employment as well as their reasons for separation.

Your chef should have lots of input on the items featured in the menu. She should understand your restaurant's concept and prepare items accordingly, with adequate attention to presentation, taste, and cost effectiveness. As a best practice, don't let your menu or your chef grow stale, but have a set schedule—every month or every two months perhaps—for your chef to create two or three new items for your menu. This routine will keep your repeat customers from growing bored while keeping your chef's creative gears turning.

In addition to the menu, your chef should have some authority over his supporting personnel. If he's worked with the same sous chef for several years and wishes to continue working with him, then you're doing your restaurant a tremendous disservice by insisting on your own staff selections. Routines, rhythms, and communication styles that develop between culinary professionals take time to mature. If you hire your chef's key coterie—up to and including, sous chef, pantry chef, saute chef, and even wait staff—you may find a better return on your investment. Again, seeing as you will be endowing your executive chef with much executive power, it's important to ensure that the two of you trust and understand one another.

If you find yourself in a position where you need to replace your existing executive chef, be careful how you do it. Many chefs, upon finding out that you're on the hunt for someone new will quit and leave your restaurant in chaos. Rather than a newspaper ad or internet posting, one of the most subtle ways of searching for a replacement chef is by using a professional headhunter. Headhunting services don't usually charge you until they've filled your position with a viable candidate. If you can hire from within you should. It's often a lot easier and less expensive than bringing someone in from the outside, and it boosts morale among your existing staff.

The median salary for an executive chef in the US is about 70K, with the lower 10% making 50K and the upper 10% making 90K. Your executive chef is a major investment, a major collaborator, and one of the principle make-or-break factors that will determine the success or failure of your restaurant.

Chapter 4: Hiring Reliable Restaurant Staff

Restaurants do not run on chefs alone. From the busboy to the general manager, there's a whole lot of teamwork involved. You've also got your line cooks, bartenders (if you have a bar), and wait staff to find and hire, so you need to get cracking. Numerically speaking, your total payroll expense should be 24 to 35% of your total gross sales.

As with any business, finding good help isn't easy. You need to do everything you can to thoroughly vet potential employees. You do this by reviewing resumes, applications, and contacting references. It's important to have everyone fill out an application, even if you're hiring someone you already know. The application serves as both a vetting tool and a contract that authorizes you to terminate employment if an employee is found to have misrepresented themselves or their qualifications and experience on their resume. You should also check resumes alongside the information presented on applications to ensure consistency. If you don't have time to thoroughly vet every prospective employee on your own, then consider investing in a service that provides background checks. Put the effort into hiring right and you'll save yourself time and expense in the long run.

Your most important hire, next to your executive chef, is your manager(s). Restaurant managers supervise the rest of the staff and must be able to make important decisions affecting the day-to-day operations of the restaurant. Restaurant managers must deal with vendors and suppliers as well, making sure that the wholesale products coming into the restaurant are the right products at the right quantity. Your manager(s) should be able to present themselves to your guests in a favorable manner, as they will be largely responsible for resolving customer complaints.

Expect to pay 35K to 55K annually for an experienced manager, plus a performance based bonus. If you're just opening up, you may be able to hire a manager who will be compensated largely based on a profit share. This will give your manager a terrific incentive to work hard towards the success of the restaurant. Another great way to invest your managers in the fate of the business is by having them start a month or so before the restaurant opens. If they contribute their own sweat to setting up the restaurant, they'll feel a higher level of pride and personal attachment to the outcome. If you do decide to compensate your managers by way of a profit share, be sure to be clear about the arrangement. They shouldn't have to wait until the restaurant achieves a net profit in order to be paid. A best practice is to have their profit share determined on a month by month basis, accounting for all monthly fixed and variable costs.

For bussing and wait staff, minimum wage is usually acceptable as these employees will receive a large amount of their incomes by way of tips. The wait staff will, of course, earn tips directly from the guests while the bus staff will usually earn tips from a daily tip-out. A tip-out is when the wait staff takes a fixed percentage of their tips for the day and pools it together to tip the busboys. You also want to take all possible measures to insure that tip income is being reported to the IRS. You can do this by requiring the wait staff to report their tips and tip-outs on paper after each shift. Your wait staff is your front line when it comes to customer interaction. They must be organized and able to work under pressure without getting flustered. The so-called "Swan Theory" is especially relevant when it comes to selecting good service staff. Like a swan who glides serenely upon the surface of the water, a good waiter or waitress must appear on the surface to be as polished and graceful. And as the swan is paddling furiously and frantically just under the water line, a good waiter or waitress must constantly be exerting her best efforts to stay organized, attentive, and friendly without appearing to be stressed. You should also prepare for dividing your wait staff into tiers, making sure that your most competent wait staff members are on the floor during your biggest rushes.

Cooks assist the chef in preparing and presenting food. The number of full-time cooks you need will depend on your budget, the complexity of your menu, and the requirements of your executive chef. You can also hire part-time cooks to work during the restaurant's busiest periods. Good full-time cooks will usually require somewhere between $575 to $650 a week to retain, which is considerably less expensive than your chef. If your menu is complex and you want to really motivate your cooks to consistently strive for excellence in their work quality, then consider coming up with a bonus or profit share opportunity that rewards them for excellent performance.

When your restaurant is first getting off the ground, you may want to consider investing in more experienced personnel so you don't have to invest so much time into training. As your restaurant matures however, you should be in a position to welcome applicants with less industry experience by developing effective internal training systems.

Chapter 5: How to Maximize Marketing Efforts

The cheapest and most effective way to market your restaurant is to ensure that every guest who dines with you has nothing short of an amazing experience from start to finish. Keeping a customer is much less expensive than finding a new customer and bad word-of-mouth spreads just as fast, if not faster, than positive word-of-mouth. Research conducted by the National Restaurant Association reveals that four out of five consumers choose to dine at a restaurant they've never visited before on the basis of a positive recommendation from a friend or family member.

While it may be unrealistic to assume that you or your staff members will never make any mistakes when it comes to delivering great food and great service, it still holds to reason that consistency is a value that should be sought after militantly by every restaurateur. Usually smaller restaurants don't purchase big media ads, but if you pay attention to the ad campaigns of major chain restaurants, you'll see that their objective really isn't to try and convince the market of their superior food, but to instead convince the market of their unwavering consistency. McDonald's, which advertises extensively, certainly doesn't have the best hamburgers, but they do have a hamburger that's unique and more or less consistent with every visit. Customers are retained on the basis of consistent experiences, and one of the major factors which will dissuade customers from trying out your restaurant will be their uncertainty. Therefore, you must stop at nothing to ensure that the experience guests have in your restaurant is a good one and consistent one. Consistency and quality are the backbone of your marketing plan.

You have other avenues as well when it comes to getting the word out. Contests, coupons, and other promotions can help. Before you invest in any outside marketing though, you should know a little about your customer base. Demographics change over time, so make sure you're making decisions based on current data. If your restaurant is located in a largely Latino area, then you need to construct marketing campaigns that reach this demographic, i.e. ads on Hispanic radio stations or television networks. If you want to advertise on the radio, call a radio station that caters to your target demographic and offer a promotional dinner for two as a prize for a contest. During the course of the contest, make sure your restaurant's name, location, and signature dish is mentioned several times on the air. For example your prize could be a dinner for two from "Charlie's, home of the Mighty Spicy Buffalo Wings." Getting this association fixed in the consumer consciousness will automatically generate a degree of familiarity between your potential customers and your restaurant. From there, you must continue to nurture this positive familiarity by ensuring that the customers who visit your restaurant leave delighted by the experience.

Something else to keep in mind—a lot of restaurants enjoy a surge of business after they first open up. You will likely be overwhelmed at times and it will be difficult to ensure the quality of every guest's experience. Meanwhile you'll be generating a lot of cash and will be tempted to spend with more profligacy. *Don't.* A restaurant's success is not measured by its early months. Even if you're delivering the goods for your guests, that fresh-on-the-scene surge will wane in time and you'll be forced to prove you're more than just a flash in the pan. Save your money for the long haul and think marathon not sprint.

Conclusion

If you follow the recommendations in this book your chances of realizing a profit with your restaurant in a short amount of time will go up. In order to make sure that you're profitable within the first year, you'll need to make sure that the profit you're generating on a monthly basis accounts for at least $1/12^{th}$ of your total start-up expense. Look for ways you can make the numbers work better on either side of the sales/cost equation. Can you choose a location with a lower rent without compromising your restaurant's profitability? Can you take more aggressive marketing steps to generate more business? Does the location you're considering have the seating capacity to maximize your sales during your busiest hours, and if not, can you find a location that will permit your restaurant to realize its full potential?

If you want to achieve quick profitability, then don't deviate from your operations budget, even if you find yourself flush with fresh cash after your first month in business. You will likely have some debt to pay off, so don't go crazy with new expenditures. Trust the work you did during the planning process. There will be a time to invest in the new tropical fish tank and the hand-carved Grizzly Bear wood sculpture, but first you need to pay back your investors. Don't get carried away early on or you'll live to regret it.

Hitting your profit goals is the culmination of many small decisions made smartly. Again, the recurring theme is *consistency*. If you have the energy and work ethic to consistently pay attention and respond intelligently to the decisions and challenges you encounter while launching your restaurant, then it is entirely possible for you to realize profitability quickly, even within the first year. Good luck!

Finally, I'd like to thank you for purchasing this book! If you enjoyed it or found it helpful, I'd greatly appreciate it if you'd take a moment to leave a review on Amazon. Thank you!

43746692R00024

Made in the USA
San Bernardino, CA
26 December 2016